THE NEW ORLEANS SAINTS

Sloan MacRae

PowerKiDS press

New York

Published in 2011 by The Rosen Publishing Group, Inc.
29 East 21st Street, New York, NY 10010

First Edition

Editor: Amelie von Zumbusch
Book Design: Greg Tucker
Layout Design: Julio Gil

Photo Credits: Cover (Drew Brees) Andy Lyons/Getty Images; cover (Reggie Bush) pp. 7, 21, 22 (top) Al Messerschmidt/Getty Images; cover (Archie Manning), p. 13 Focus on Sport/Getty Images; cover (background), p. 9 Scott Boehm/Getty Images; p. 5 Donald Miralle/Getty Images; p. 11 John D. Hanlon/Sports Illustrated/Getty Images; pp. 15, 22 (middle) George Rose/Getty Images; p. 17 Dave Einsel/Getty Images; p. 19 Doug Benc/Getty Images; p. 22 (bottom) Mario Tama/Getty Images.

Library of Congress Cataloging-in-Publication Data

MacRae, Sloan.
 The New Orleans Saints / by Sloan MacRae. — 1st ed.
     p. cm. — (America's greatest teams)
 Includes index.
 ISBN 978-1-4488-2578-3 (library binding) — ISBN 978-1-4488-2745-9 (pbk.) —
ISBN 978-1-4488-2746-6 (6-pack)
 1. New Orleans Saints (Football team)—History—Juvenile literature. I. Title. II. Series.
 GV956.N366M35 2011
 796.332′640976335—dc22

                                        2010034812

Manufactured in the United States of America

CPSIA Compliance Information: Batch #WW11PK: For Further Information contact Rosen Publishing, New York, New York at 1-800-237-9932

CONTENTS

AMERICA'S NEW TEAM

The New Orleans Saints have not always been one of the most successful teams in **professional** football. However, they are one of the most loved. The Saints struggled for many years. In fact, it took them over 40 years to reach their first **Super Bowl**.

The people of New Orleans, Louisiana, are part of what makes the team great. New Orleans **fans** stood by the Saints through many long, losing seasons. The Saints came through for their city when the people of New Orleans most needed a winning team. Many football fans believe the New Orleans Saints are **heroes**. Some even came to call the Saints America's Team.

The Saints won their first Super Bowl in 2010. Tracy Porter (center) made a great interception, or catch of a ball thrown by the other team's quarterback.

WHEN THE SAINTS GO MARCHING IN

The Saints play in a **stadium** called the Superdome. It is in New Orleans. New Orleans is famous for its French history and its jazz music. The Saints get their name from a very famous jazz song, called "When the Saints Go Marching In." When people hear this song, they think of New Orleans.

Football teams have letters or pictures called **logos** that help fans tell different teams apart. The Saints' logo is a fleur-de-lis. The fleur-de-lis is a very old French **symbol**. It is also one of the symbols for New Orleans. The Saints' colors are black, gold, and white.

In this picture, you can see the Saints' fleur-de-lis logo on the helmet and shoulders of Saints player Reggie Bush.

WHO DAT?

Saints fans love their team, even though the Saints lost for many seasons. New Orleans fans like to yell "Who dat?" in the Superdome during home games. This comes from a longer **chant** that goes, "Who dat say dey gonna beat dem Saints?"

Saints fans are sometimes called the Who Dat Nation or even Who Dats. Saints players also like to yell "Who dat?" at games. The "Who dat" chant is such a hit with the Saints' fans that fans from other teams have started using it. Saints fans also love the song "When the Saints Go Marching In."

The Superdome's full name is the Louisiana Superdome. The Saints played their first game there in 1975.

A SLOW START

The New Orleans Saints were formed in the fall of 1966. They played their first game almost a year later, in 1967. Many new National Football **League**, or NFL, teams struggle in their first seasons. The Saints certainly did. In fact, they won only three games in their first season.

The next few seasons also went poorly. The people of New Orleans were glad to have a football team. However, their team was one of the worst in the NFL. It would take the Saints 20 years to change this. They finally recorded a winning season in 1987.

Billy Kilmer (center) was one of the New Orleans Saints' first quarterbacks. He played for the team between 1967 and 1970.

THE AIN'TS

Though the Saints did not have a great record in their early years, they did have some of the NFL's best players. **Quarterback** Archie Manning joined the team in 1971. He was one of the greatest college football players of all time. He did his best to lead the Saints. It takes more than a few good players to make a team great, though.

The Saints were so bad over the years that some fans began to nickname the team the Ain'ts. Many fans even wore paper bags over their heads during games. Most Saints fans stood by their team even through those bad seasons.

Archie Manning (right) is the father of Indianapolis Colts quarterback Peyton Manning and New York Giants quarterback Eli Manning.

ALMOST THERE

In 1986, the Saints got a new head **coach** named Jim Mora. Mora knew how to win football games. He turned the team around. The Saints finally won more games than they lost during the 1987 season. They lost only three games. They reached the **play-offs** for the first time during that same season.

The Saints made the play-offs again in the 1990, 1991, and 1992 seasons. The team played well in the regular season, but they struggled in the play-offs. They did not win one play-off game with Mora as head coach. They were now a good team. However, they were not quite a great team yet.

Jim Mora led the Saints to become a much better team. Mora was named the NFL's coach of the year after the Saints' great 1987 season.

HURRICANE KATRINA

A powerful storm called **Hurricane** Katrina struck New Orleans in the late summer of 2005. The storm caused a flood that destroyed much of the city. Hundreds of people died. Thousands more lost their homes. The city opened the Superdome as a place to supply food, water, and safety to thousands of people.

Hurricane Katrina damaged the Superdome badly. The stadium closed for a whole season. The Saints played at stadiums in Baton Rouge, Louisiana, and San Antonio, Texas. It looked like New Orleans might never come back from the storm. For now, football was the last thing on fans' minds.

There was not enough food or water for the people in the Superdome during Hurricane Katrina. Several days passed before help came.

SEAN PAYTON AND DREW BREES

In time, people returned to New Orleans and began to rebuild the city. They needed heroes, and the Saints were ready. A new head coach named Sean Payton and a new quarterback named Drew Brees joined the team in 2006. They knew that the city needed the Saints to win.

The team had its best season yet in 2009. The Saints won their first 13 games and went on to beat the Indianapolis Colts in the Super Bowl. The city of New Orleans had almost been destroyed. Now it had its first NFL **championship**. Football fans all across America began rooting for the Saints.

Drew Brees proudly held up the Vince Lombardi Trophy after the Saints' Super Bowl win. They beat the Colts, 31–17.

STILL MARCHING

Saints fans remained true to their team, even when it struggled. The team paid them back by coming through for the city in its darkest moments. The Saints' Super Bowl win lifted the spirits of fans who were still shaken after Hurricane Katrina.

The Saints stood by New Orleans off the field, too. Brees bought a house there shortly after joining the team. He believed in the community. He knew it could come back from Katrina.

Today, the Saints have many great players, such as Brees, Jahri Evans, and Darren Sharper. At long last, the Saints are one of the NFL's best teams.

Jahri Evans (left) plays guard for the Saints. He joined the team in 2006. Since then, Evans has become one of the top guards in the NFL.

NEW ORLEANS SAINTS TIMELINE

1966

The city of New Orleans gets an NFL team.

1967

The Saints lose to the Los Angeles Rams in their first regular-season game.

1970

The Saints' Tom Dempsey sets an NFL record for the longest field goal kick, at 63 yards. Dempsey was born without toes on his right foot.

1987

The Saints record their first winning season.

1996

Head coach Jim Mora, who led the Saints to their first play-off appearance, steps down.

2000

The Saints win for the first time in the play-offs, when they beat the St. Louis Rams.

2005

Hurricane Katrina hits New Orleans.

2006

The Saints play their first game in the Superdome since Hurricane Katrina. They beat the Atlanta Falcons.

2010

The Saints beat the Indianapolis Colts and win their first Super Bowl.

GLOSSARY

CHAMPIONSHIP (CHAM-pee-un-ship) Official naming of the best or winner.

CHANT (CHANT) Saying words over and over again without changing tone.

COACH (KOHCH) A person who directs a team.

FANS (FANZ) People who watch a sport or a game.

HEROES (HEER-ohz) People who are looked up to by other people.

HURRICANE (HUR-ih-kayn) A storm with strong winds and heavy rain.

LEAGUE (LEEG) A group of sports teams.

LOGOS (LOH-gohz) Pictures, words, or letters that stand for a team or company.

PLAY-OFFS (PLAY-ofs) Games played after the regular season ends to see who will play in the championship game.

PROFESSIONAL (pruh-FESH-nul) Having players who are paid.

QUARTERBACK (KWAHR-ter-bak) A football player who directs the team's plays.

STADIUM (STAY-dee-um) A place where sports are played.

SUPER BOWL (SOO-per BOHL) The championship game of NFL football.

SYMBOL (SIM-bul) An object or a picture that stands for something else.

INDEX

WEB SITES

Due to the changing nature of Internet links, PowerKids Press has developed an online list of Web sites related to the subject of this book. This site is updated regularly. Please use this link to access the list:
www.powerkidslinks.com/teams/fsaints/